20TH CENTURY AMERICAN COMPOSERS
Upper Intermediate Level Piano

27 Works by 8 Composers

Samuel Barber • Dave Brubeck • Norman Dello Joio • Charles T. Griffes
Robert Muczynski • Alexander Tcherepnin • William Schuman • Virgil Thomson

ISBN 978-1-4950-0826-9

ED 4606

G. SCHIRMER, Inc.

DISTRIBUTED BY

HAL•LEONARD®
CORPORATION
7777 W. BLUEMOUND RD. P.O. BOX 13819 MILWAUKEE, WI 53213

www.musicsalesclassical.com
www.halleonard.com

CONTENTS

NOTES ON THE MUSIC

Samuel Barber (1910–1981)

FRESH FROM WEST CHESTER (SOME JAZZINGS)
Poison Ivy (1925)
Let's Sit It Out; I'd Rather Watch (1926)

THREE ESSAYS (1926)

Born in Pennsylvania, Samuel Barber was a precocious musical talent who at fourteen began studies in voice, piano, and composition at the Curtis Institute. One of the most prominent American composers of the 20th century, he is remembered for his idiosyncratic, neo-Romantic style. Early in his career he performed as a singer, which may have helped him develop an aptitude for writing the soaring melodic lines that define his instrumental works. Barber wrote for orchestra, voice, choir, piano, chamber ensemble, and solo instruments and was well acclaimed during his lifetime. After 1938, almost all of his compositions were written on commission from renowned performers and ensembles.[1] Among his well-known pieces are the *Adagio for Strings* (1936), the opera *Vanessa* (1956–57), *Knoxville: Summer of 1915* (1947), and *Hermit Songs* (1953).

The works presented here were written when Barber was still a teenager. The word "jazz" in *Fresh from West Chester (Some Jazzings)* had a different association in the mid 1920s than it does today. The word was used to describe something hip, casual, and distinctively American. The humorous titles and tempo markings conceal Barber's ambitions for the works, written in the early period of his studies with Scalero, who did not approve of the pieces. Barber grew quickly as a composer in his teenage years, and *Three Essays*, written just two years after *Fresh from West Chester*, is a clear example of his rapid progress.

[1] Barbara B. Heyman, *A Comprehensive Thematic Catalog of the Works of Samuel Barber* (New York, NY: Oxford University Press, manuscript copy consulted prior to publication).

Dave Brubeck (1920–2012)

DAD PLAYS THE HARMONICA from *Reminiscences of the Cattle Country* (1946)

Dave Brubeck was a jazz pianist, composer, and bandleader who re-popularized jazz in the 1950s and 60s, producing records that appealed to audiences who favored short and catchy pop tunes. Brubeck grew up on a farm outside of San Francisco. His father was a cattle rancher and his mother was the choir director at a Presbyterian church. His mother did not allow her children to listen to the radio, so David and his siblings took up different instruments and made their own music, learning to play classical repertoire, religious spirituals, and folk songs. Brubeck enlisted in the army during World War II and entertained European troops playing piano in an Army band. He attended Mills College on the G.I. Bill, where he studied composition with Darius Milhaud. In the late 1940s and early 50s he formed a quartet with Ron Crotty, Cal Tjader, and Paul Desmond. The group went on a successful tour of U.S. colleges and released the album *Jazz at Oberlin* which sold hundreds of thousands of copies. In 1954, the group signed a deal with Columbia Records and Brubeck became the second jazz musician to be featured on the cover of Time (the first was Louis Armstrong). His 1959 recording of Paul Desmond's "Take Five" was the first jazz instrumental single to go platinum. Brubeck continued to perform, record, and compose until his death in 2012.

Norman Dello Joio (1913–2008)

SUITE FOR PIANO (1940)

Norman Dello Joio grew up in a musical home in New York City, the son of an Italian immigrant father who worked as an organist, pianist, singer, and vocal coach. Musicians were constantly in the home, including singers from the Met who came for coaching sessions. He took organ lessons from his Godfather, Pietro Yon, a composer and the organist for St. Patrick's Cathedral. At fourteen he took his first job as organist of the Star of the Sea Church. After initial composition training at the Institute of Musical Art and the Juilliard School, Dello Joio began studying with Paul Hindemith at the Yale School of Music. Hindemith encouraged Dello Joio to embrace the lyricism of his writing, which was infused with the Italian opera and church music of his childhood, as well as early jazz. He remained true to his style in writing operas, ballets, orchestral pieces, solo instrumental works, and sacred music. In 1957, the Young Composers Project, which placed composers under the age of thirty-five as composers-in-residence of public high schools around the country, was founded based upon Dello Joio's suggestion and Dello Joio served as chairman of the project's policy committee.

Charles T. Griffes (1884–1920)
THE WHITE PEACOCK from *Roman Sketches*, Op. 7 (1915)

Charles T. Griffes was perhaps the best known American Impressionist composer. Aside from the French Impressionists, he was also influenced by German Romanticism. Later in life, he turned to more dissonant and experimental textures and tonalities. Griffes took piano lessons with Mary Selena Broughton at Elmira College as a boy, and she eventually encouraged him to move to Berlin for a formal education. He moved to Berlin in 1903 to study piano and composition at the Stern Conservatory. Originally intending to pursue a career as a concert pianist, Griffes soon became more focused on composing. He returned to the United States in 1907 and took a job as director of music at the Hackley School in Tarrytown, New York. He continued in this role until his early death at age thirty-five from influenza. Griffes composed in his free time, and the school's proximity to New York allowed him to promote his music there. "The White Peacock," a movement from *Roman Sketches*, Op. 7, shows clear influences from French Impressionism. It is one of his most popular works and he later arranged it for a ballet production.

Robert Muczynski (1929–2010)
A SUMMER JOURNAL, OP. 19 (1964)

Composer and pianist Robert Muczynski was born in Chicago and studied at DePaul University with Alexander Tcherepnin. At twenty-nine he made his Carnegie Hall debut with a performance of his own compositions. In addition to solo piano works, Muczynski mainly wrote for small chamber ensembles and also composed several orchestral pieces. His flute and saxophone sonatas, as well as *Time Pieces* for clarinet and piano, have become part of the standard repertoire for those instruments. In 1981, his concerto for saxophone was nominated for the Pulitzer Prize. Muczynski was composer in residence at the University of Arizona from 1965 until his retirement in 1988.

Alexander Tcherepnin (1889–1977)
Selections from BAGATELLES, OP. 5 (1913–1918)

Alexander Tcherepnin was born in St. Petersburg, the son of conductor and composer Nicolay Tcherepnin. Eminent Russian composers such as Rimsky-Korsakov, Stravinsky, and Prokofiev frequented his home. In 1917, following the Russian Revolution, the family moved to Tbillsi, Georgia, and then on to Paris in 1921 after the communists came to power. In Paris, Alexander studied with Isidore Philipp and composed his first large-scale works. His *Concerto da camera* for violin, flute, and chamber orchestra won the Schott prize in 1925 and brought him international recognition. Tcherepnin lived in China between 1934–37, where he studied Chinese classical music and married pianist Lee Hsien Ming. He then returned to Paris, where he remained even under the German occupation. Following World War II, he moved to Chicago to teach at DePaul University. He lived in Chicago for fifteen years, teaching and also composing some of his most important symphonic works such as the Fourth Symphony and *Symphonic Prayer*. He became a United States citizen in 1958. In 1964, he retired from DePaul and moved to New York. *Bagetelles*, Op. 5 is one of Tcherepnin's most famous works. It is based upon a number of small piano pieces, many featuring irregular rhythms and dissonant harmonies, which Tcherepnin had composed by the age of fourteen. It was first published in Paris in 1922.

William Schuman (1910–1992)
THREE-SCORE SET (1943)

William Schuman was a composer and prominent administrator in his hometown of New York City, where he had a lasting impact on some of the city's most important musical institutions. As a young man, Schuman took composition lessons with Charles Haubiel, Bernard Wagenaar, and Roy Harris. From 1935–45, he taught composition at Sarah Lawrence College. In 1937, Aaron Copland sparked a close working relationship between Schuman and the Boston Symphony Orchestra when he suggested that Schuman send his Symphony No. 2 to Serge Koussevitzky. The BSO subsequently premiered a number of Schuman's works. *A Free Song*, premiered by the BSO in 1943, won the first Pulitzer Prize ever awarded in music. In 1945, Schuman left Sarah Lawrence for a successful string of artistic management positions. The first was president of the Institute of Musical Arts and the Juilliard School, which he eventually merged into one institution. He founded the Juilliard String Quartet, the school's dance division, and also instituted a comprehensive curriculum of music history and theory. From 1962–68 he was president of Lincoln Center, where he created the Chamber Music Society, Film Society, and a summer festival that eventually became the beloved Mostly Mozart Festival. He was also responsible for bringing the New York City Opera and the New York City Ballet to Lincoln Center, and set the stage for Juilliard's eventual move to the complex. He devoted his summers to composition, writing chamber, choral, and orchestral works that were praised not only by Koussevitzky, but also by Leonard Bernstein and Aaron Copland, who in a review of his Fourth String Quartet referred to Schuman as one of the top men in American music.[1]

[1]Steve Swayne, "Schuman, William," *Grove Music Online*, Oxford Music Online, Oxford University Press, accessed November 17, 2014, http://www.oxfordmusiconline.com/subscriber/article/grove/music/A2225534.

Virgil Thomson (1896-1989)

Selections from SEVENTEEN PORTRAITS FOR PIANO

Doña Flor: Receiving (1982)

Brendan Lemon: A Study for Piano (1984)

A composer as well as a notable music critic, Virgil Thomson was born and raised in Kansas City, Missouri. His father was a farmer and later a civil servant, but his house was filled with the parlor songs and hymns that would later animate his compositions with a touch of the vernacular. He graduated from Harvard University, where he studied with Edward Burlingame Hill and A. T. Davison. He was also heavily influenced by S. Foster Damon, an English professor, who introduced him to the music of Erik Satie and to Gertrude Stein's writing. In 1925, following graduate studies at Juilliard, he moved to Paris and studied with Nadia Boulanger. He remained in Paris for fifteen years, and met both Satie and Stein, two important artistic influences on his work. He became especially close to Stein, setting her poetry and prose to music and collaborating with her on two operas. Offered a job as chief music critic at the *Herald Tribune*, Thomson returned to the United States in 1940. He was famous for his literary and polemic style and continued to compose, conduct, and publish his own works. In 1949, he won a Pulitzer Prize for the soundtrack to the film *Louisiana Story*.

Fresh from West Chester
(Some Jazzings)

I. Poison Ivy

Samuel Barber
July, 1925

Allegro, as a dog wags his tail

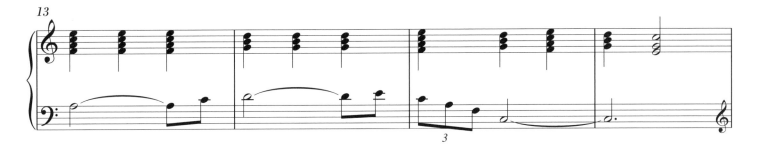

On the cover of the manuscript Barber wrote: "A country-dance that isn't. Accredited to, and blamed on T.T. Garboriasky
—July 1925."

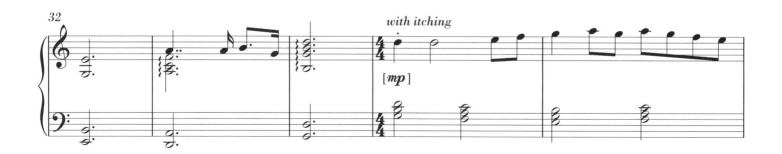

Bad memories

II. Let's Sit It Out; I'd Rather Watch

A Walls*

Samuel Barber
May, 1926

[**Waltz**]

On the cover of the manuscript, Barber wrote: "I, Sam Barber, did it with my little hatchet—May, 1926."

* "A Walls" is a play on the word "waltz."

**Barber indicated few dynamics in this piece. We have made minimal suggestions.

***The manuscript has F3 and A3 on the second and third beats of the left hand diad; editorial choice is to match measure 89, where the manuscript clearly has F and B.

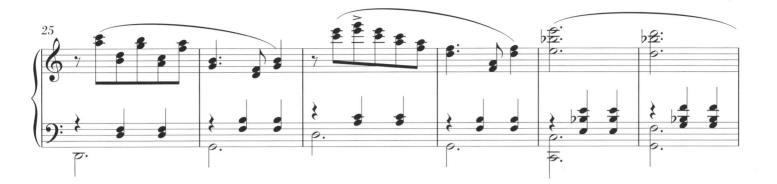

flirtatiously, molto koketto*

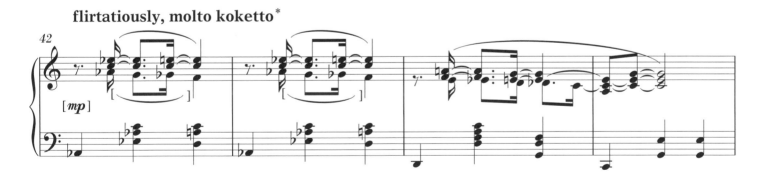

*Barber made up this word.

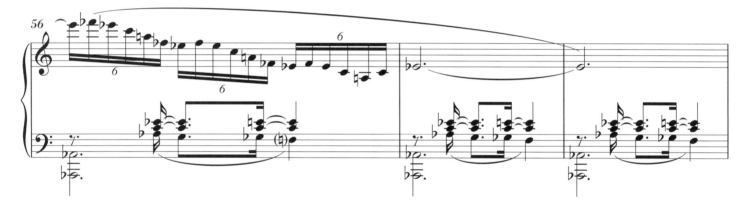

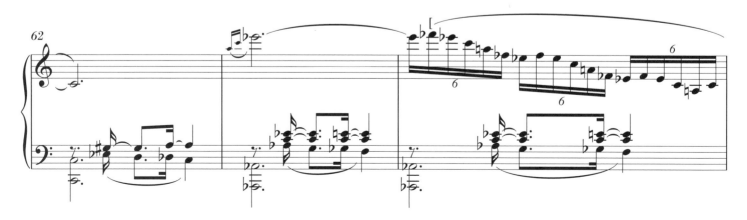

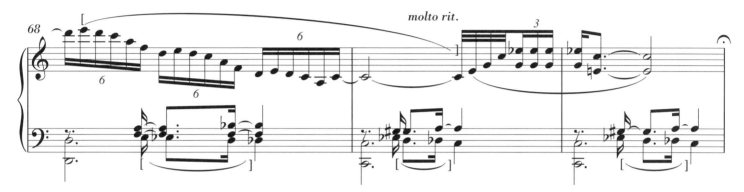

*Barber's manuscript indicates a low G natural on the downbeat of measure 80. We believe this to be a mistake, and have matched measure 51. Another discrepancy in the same measure, right hand, has been corrected to match measure 51.

Tempo I

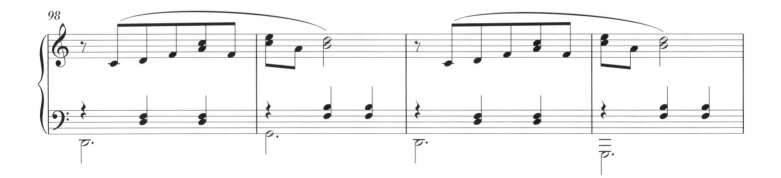

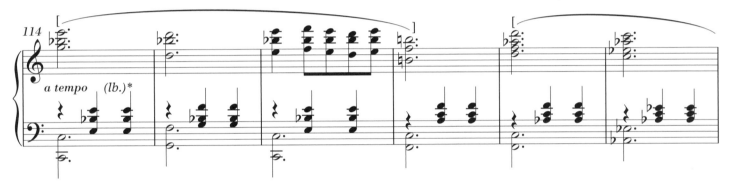

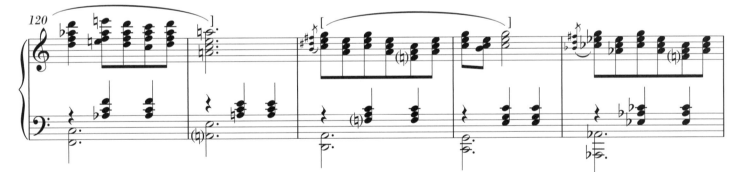

*This mysterious indication appears thus in the manuscript. In an alternate copy of this movement owned by the late Paul Wittke, Barber's editor at G. Schirmer, the direction "pound keys" appears after *(lb)*. It is unclear if the words were added by Wittke or Barber.

At the end of the manuscript Barber wrote: "Soon to be released—*Curtis Institute Blues—The Piece that makes People Pray*."

Essay I
for Piano

Samuel Barber
completed June 5, 1926

Andante e sostenuto

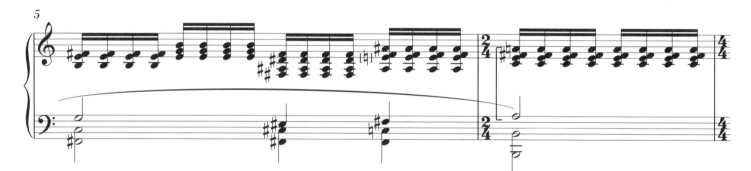

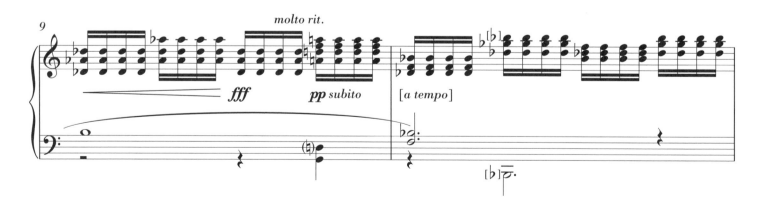

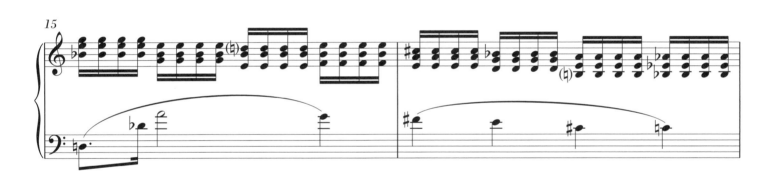

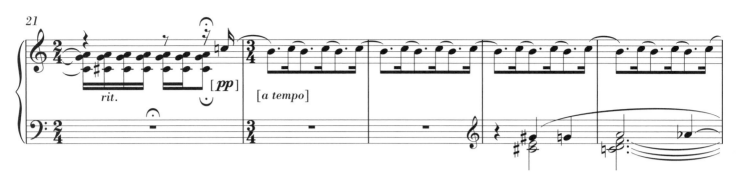

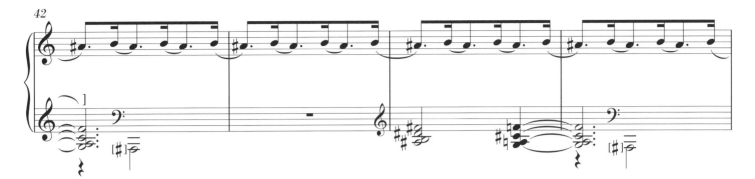

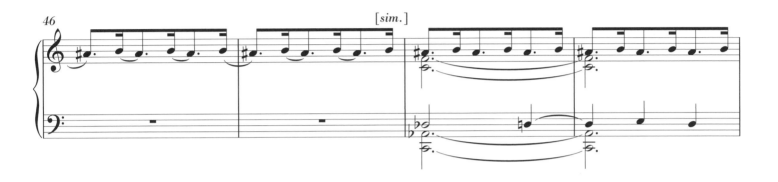

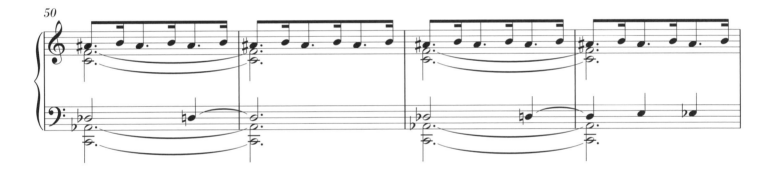

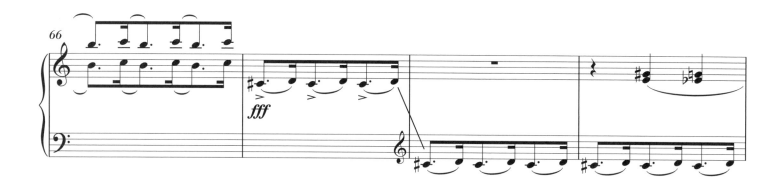

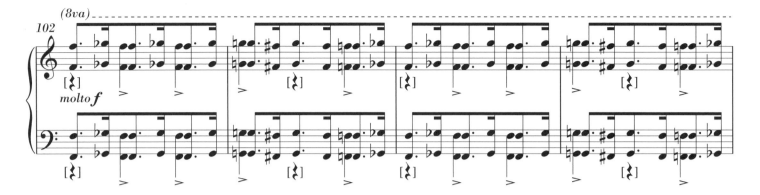

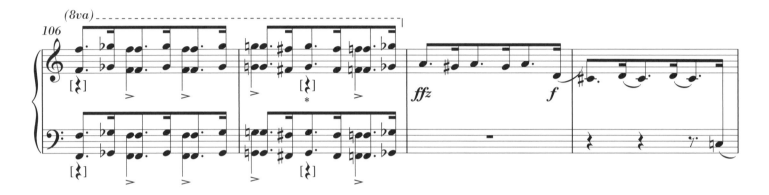

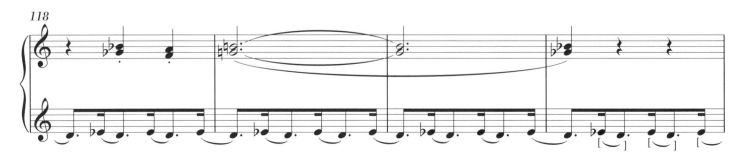

*Barber indicated a quarter note in the right hand on beat two of this measure. As no corresponding note appears in the left hand, no accent appears on the note, and the pattern remains consistent to this point, the editors have omitted the note.

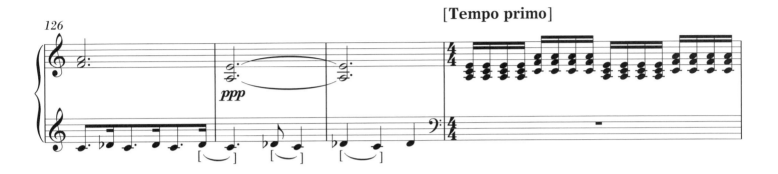

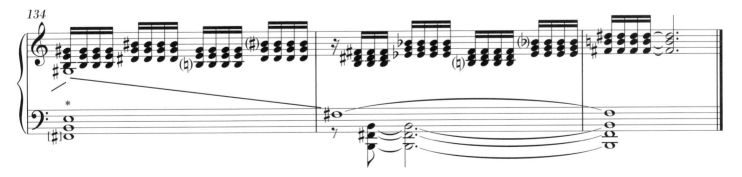

*The low note F-sharp is an editorial guess. No ♯ appears before the low F in the manuscript, nor does a ♮. If Barber had intended a ♮ in this context, we reckon that he would have deliberately indicated it.

Essay II
for Piano

Samuel Barber
July, 1926

Allegro molto

*Barber clearly indicated E-natural in his manuscript when this material later recurs.
**The pattern would suggest the note F-sharp in the left hand; Barber's manuscript has G-sharp.

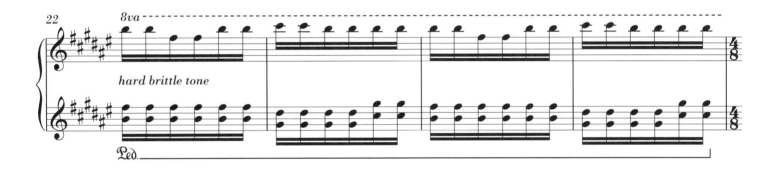

*Barber's manuscript indicates a B-natural in the left hand chord. We believe this is an error and have matched measure 127.

[*staccato sempre*]

mf *legato*

8va

*This chord is written as a quarter note in the manuscript, likely an error.

**The left hand of this measure is written an octave higher in the manuscript. Barber writes "8va bassa" below.
 We have notated it as such, an octave lower. Because of context, we assume this refers only to measure 51.

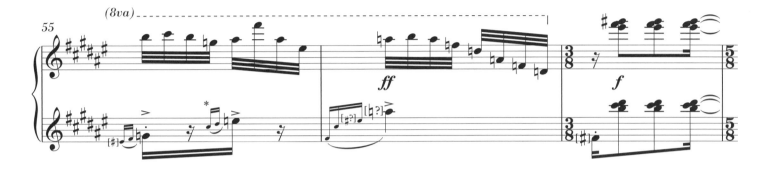

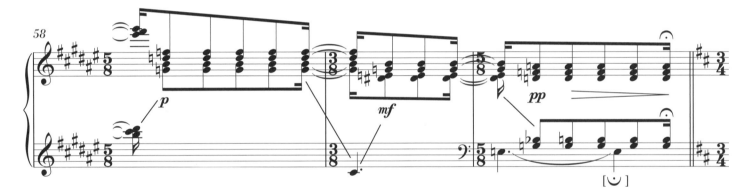

*The manuscript is unclear on the second figure in the left hand. Printed is our best guess of Barber's intention.
**"Lenápe"—a region of the country largely in Delaware, New Jersey, New York, and Pennsylvania named for the Lenape Indian tribe that inhabited this area, a likely reference to Lake Lenape Park, a local weekend get-away spot about 40 miles north of where Barber grew up.

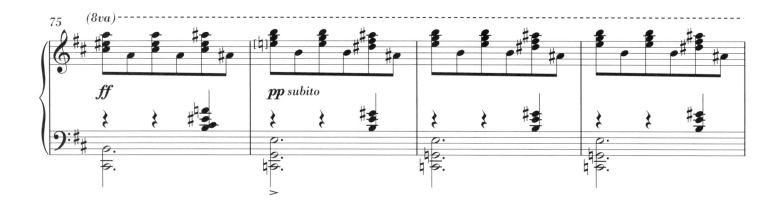

Tempo I

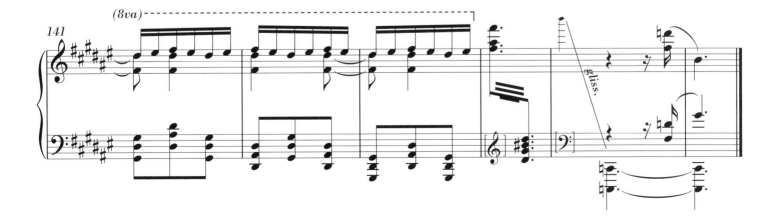

Essay III
for Piano

Samuel Barber
completed June 30, 1926

Con moto
the theme with monotonous emphasis throughout

mf

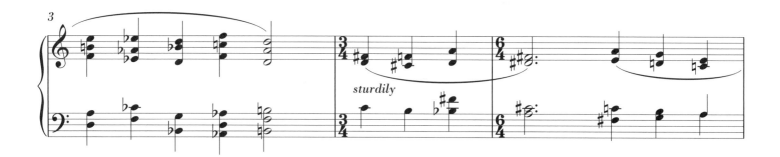

sturdily

f

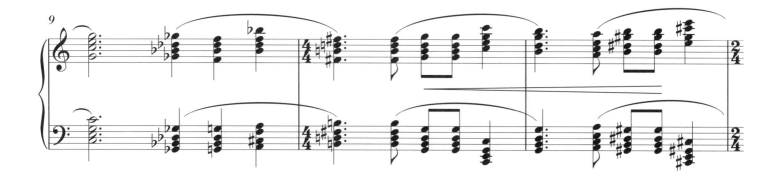

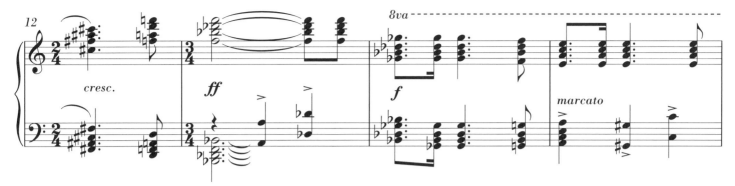

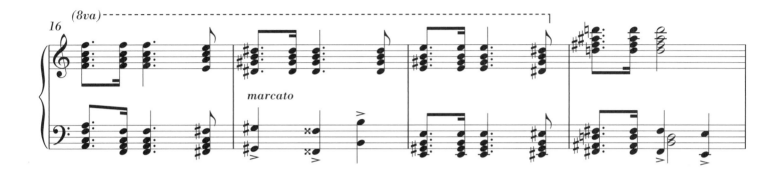

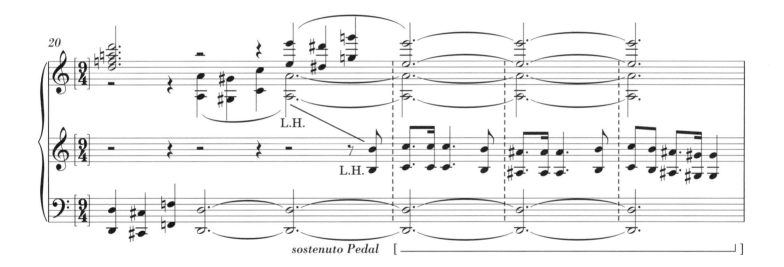

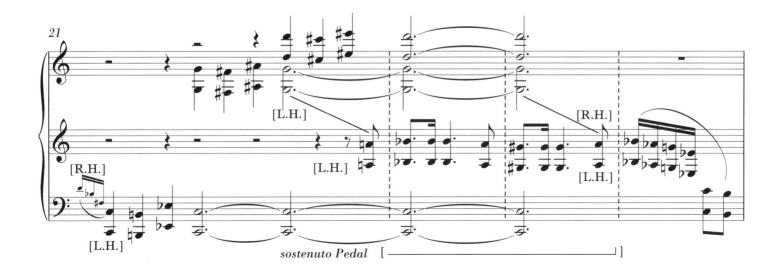

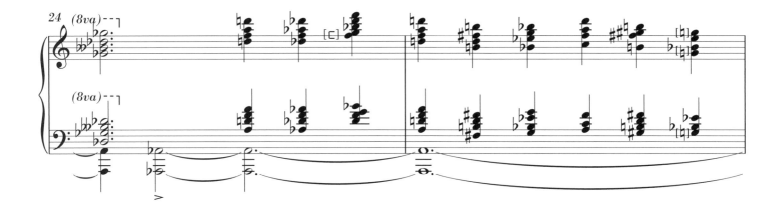

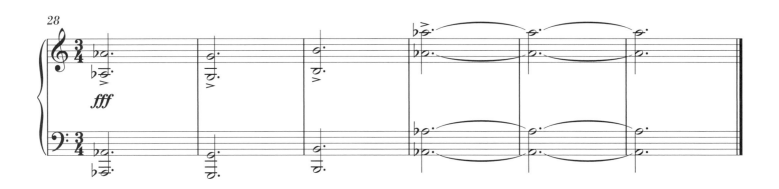

Dad Plays the Harmonica

Dave Brubeck

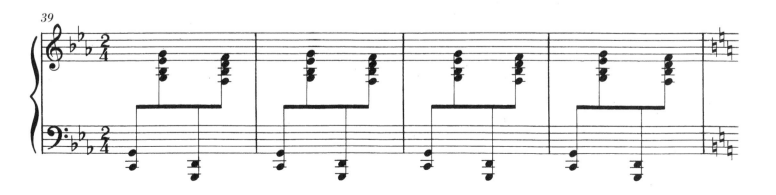

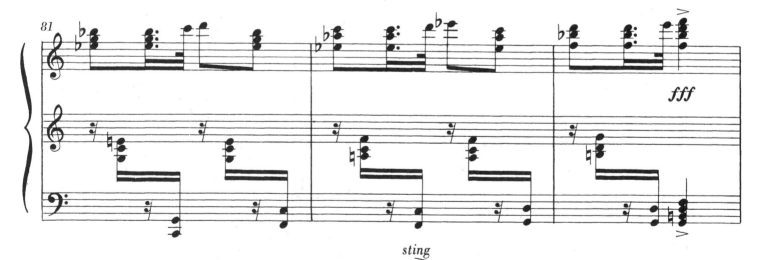

* *To be depressed, not struck by L.H.*
Let the sound emerge as the pedal is released, on both R.H. and L.H. C's.

1946, Mills College
Oakland, California

Suite for Piano

I

Norman Dello Joio

II

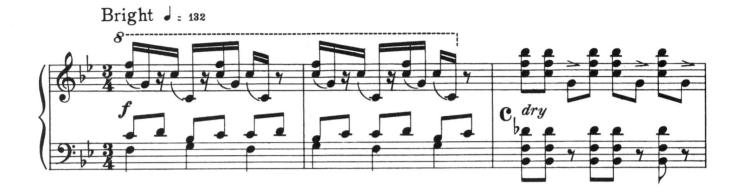

III

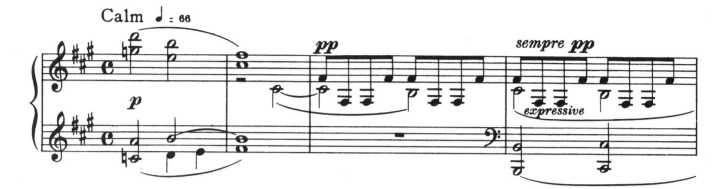

IV

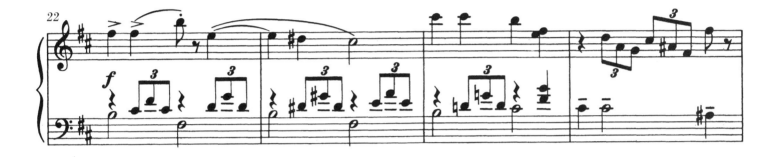

48

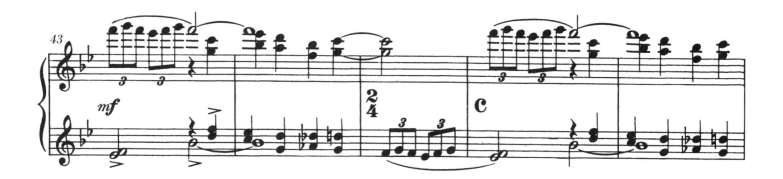

Spring 1940

To Gloria

A Summer Journal

Robert Muczynski
Op. 19

Morning Promenade

Park Scene

Midday

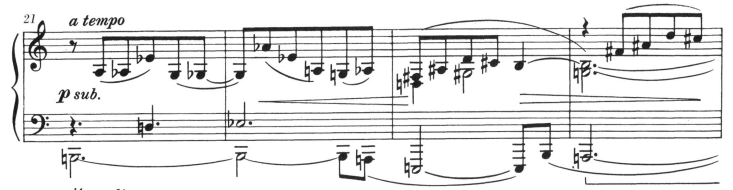

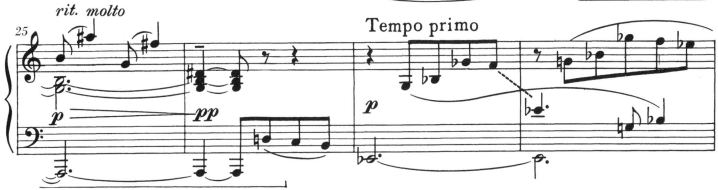

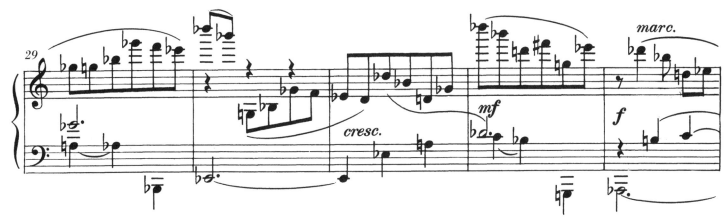

Birds

(cross over)

Solitude

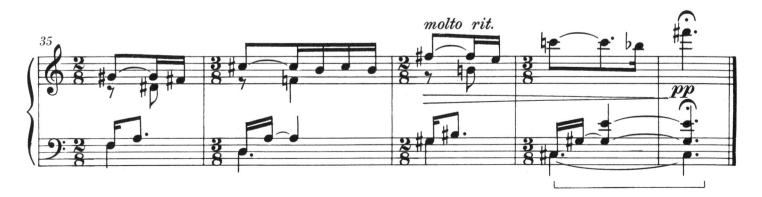

Night Rain

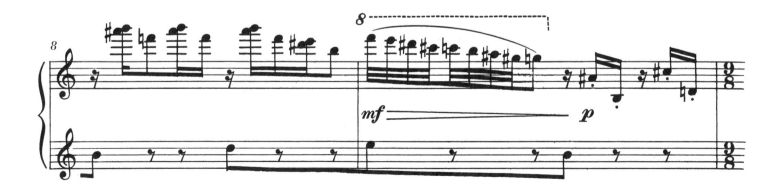

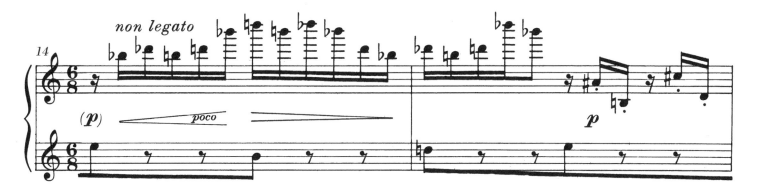

Jublilee

Allegro con spirito ♩=132 *(rhythmically; well-accented)*

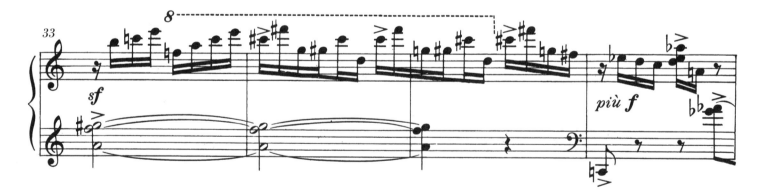

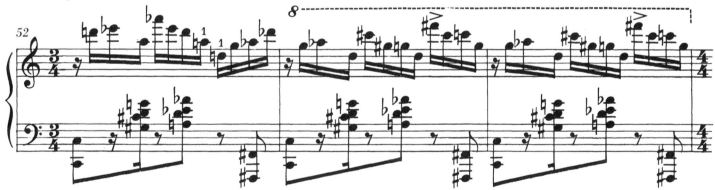

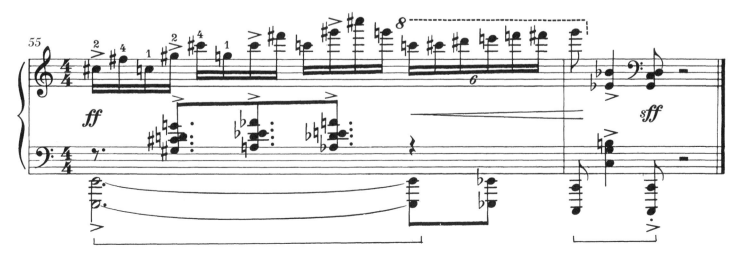

A Maika Kalamkarova

Bagatelles
(a selection)

Alexander Tcherepnin
Op. 5

1

Allegro marciale ♩ = 96

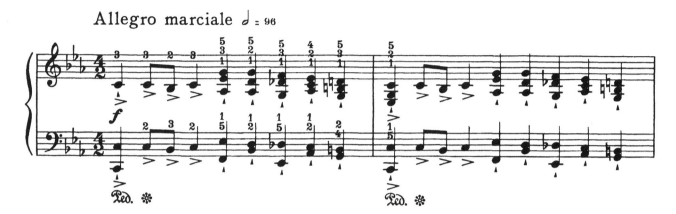

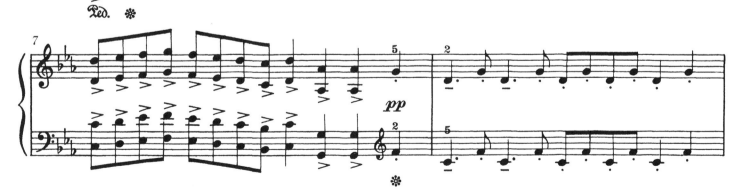

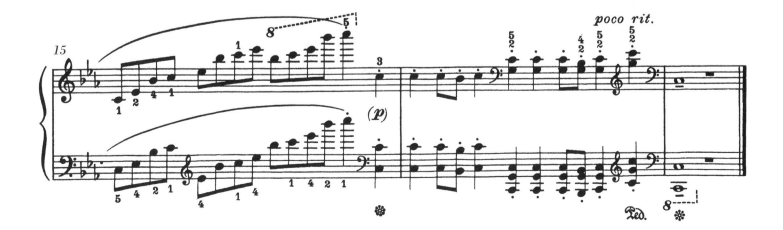

2

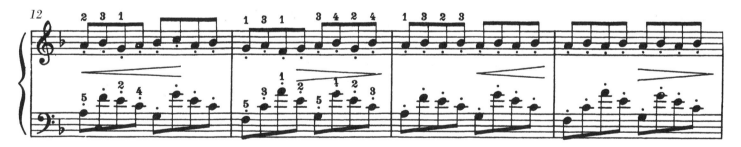

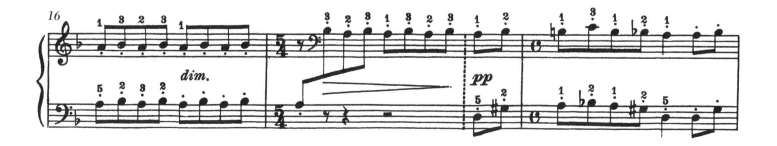

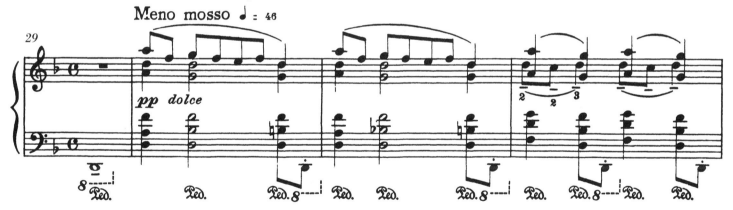

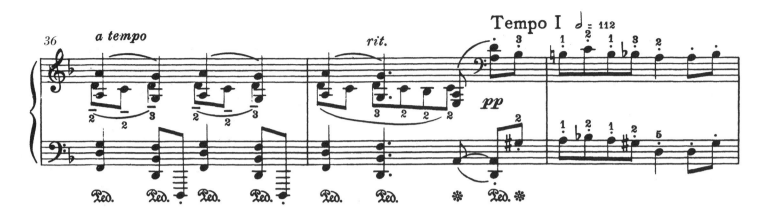

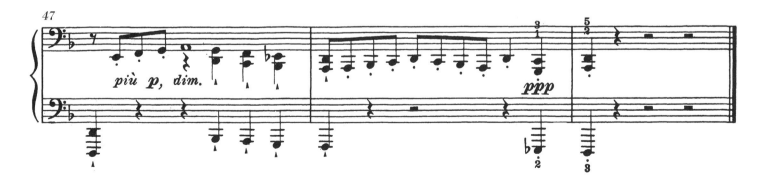

4

Lento con tristezza ♪ = 72

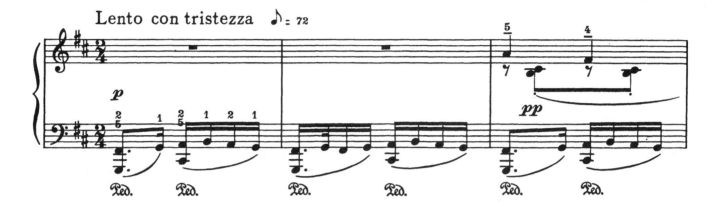

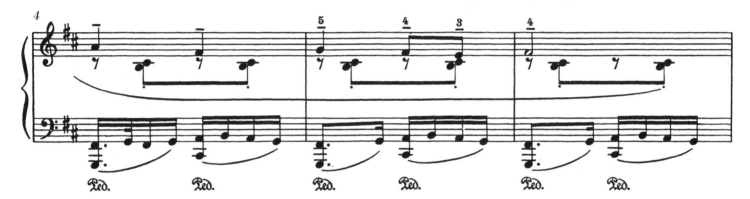

5

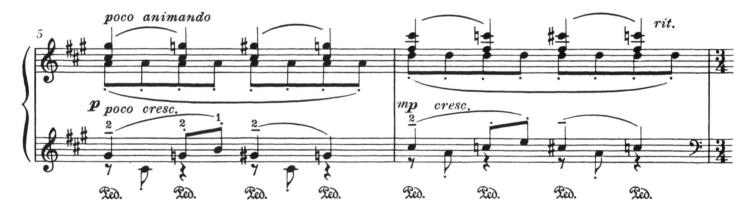

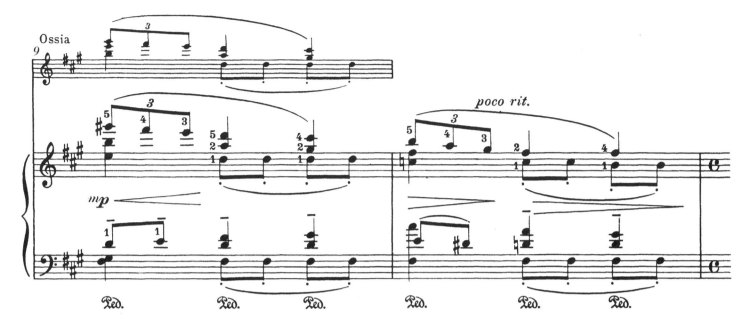

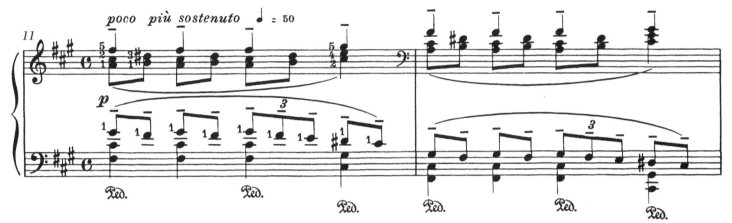

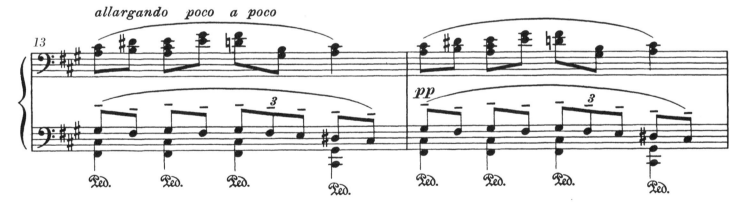

For C.E.

Three-Score Set

William Schuman

I

II

Ped. ✻

III

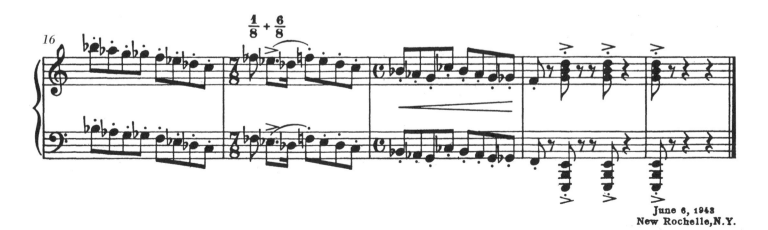

June 6, 1943
New Rochelle, N.Y.

to Rudolph Ganz

The White Peacock
from *Roman Sketches*

Charles T. Griffes
Op. 7, No.1

Languidamente e molto rubato

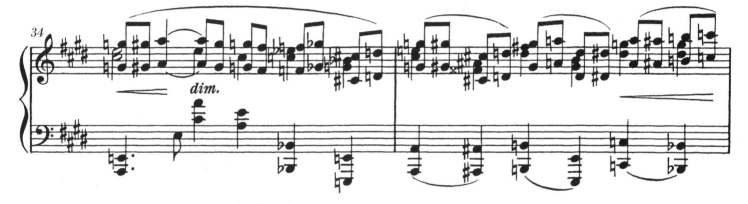

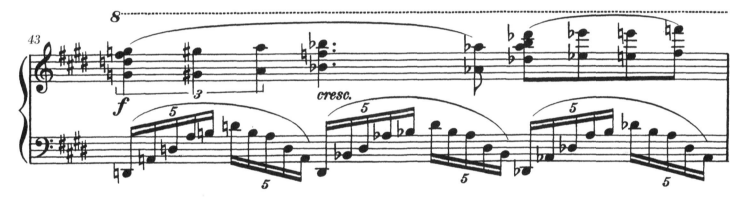

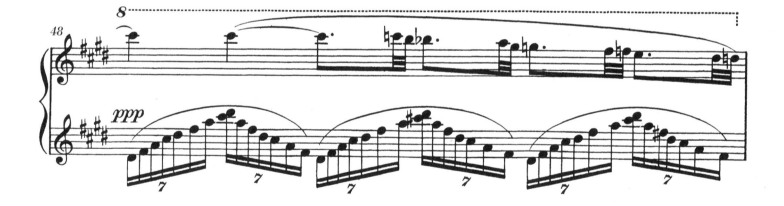

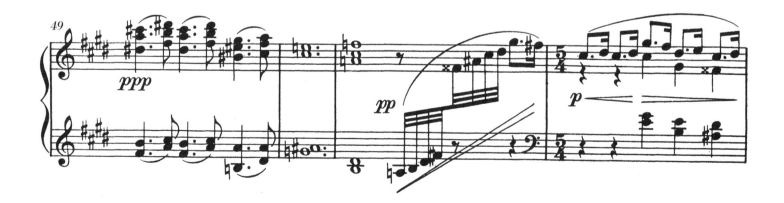

molto dim. e rit.

June, 1915

Doña Flor: Receiving
from *Seventeen Portraits for Piano*

Fingerings by
Yvar Mikhashoff

Virgil Thomson

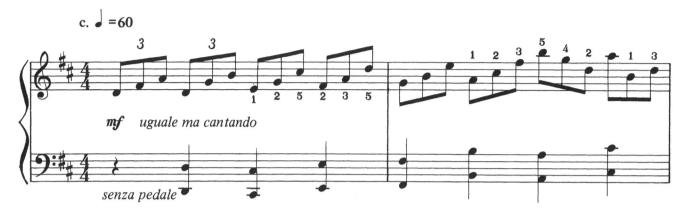

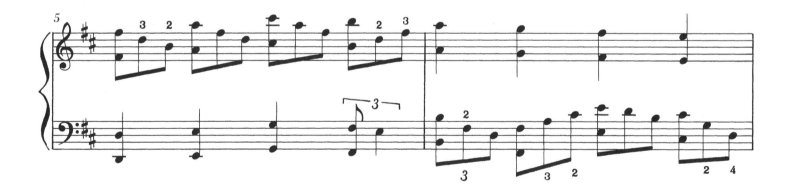

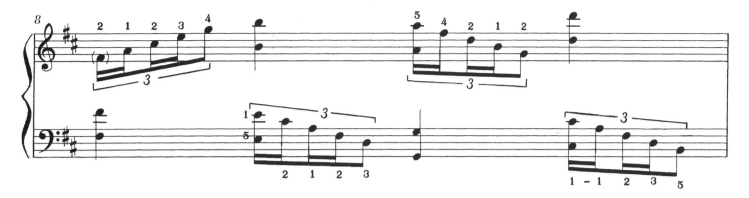

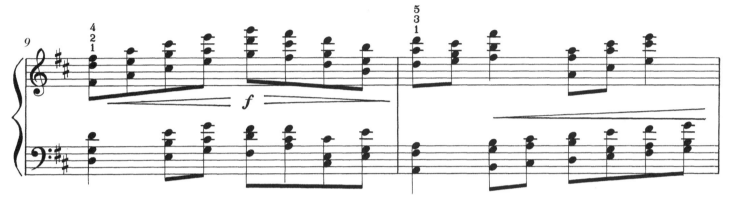

Caracas, 2 February 1982

1'

Brendan Lemon: A Study Piece for Piano
from *Seventeen Portraits for Piano*

Fingerings by
Yvar Mikhashoff

Virgil Thomson

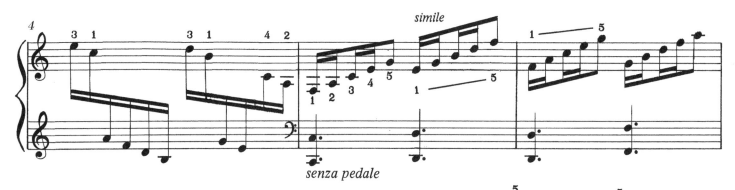

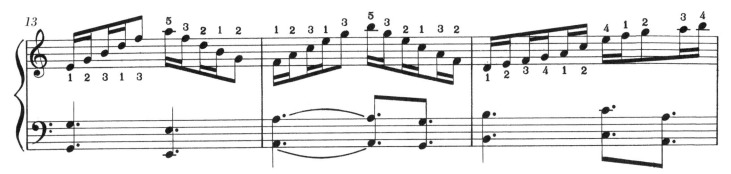

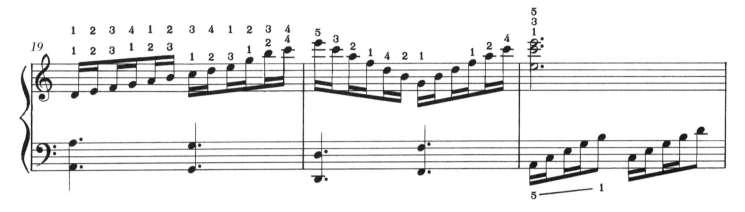

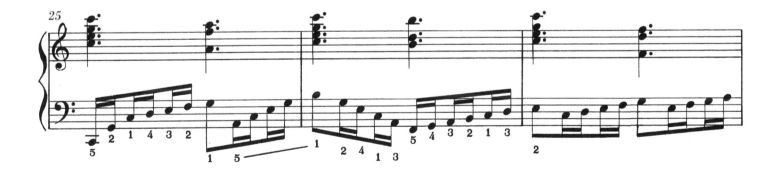

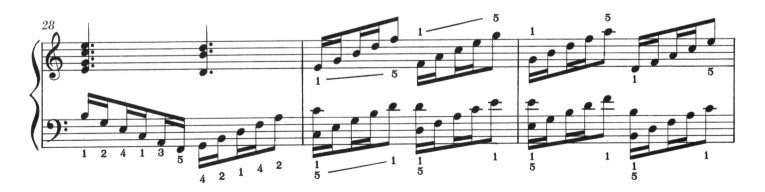

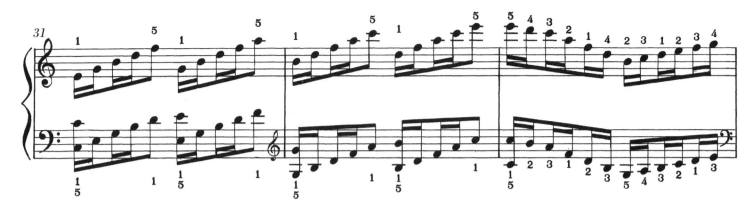

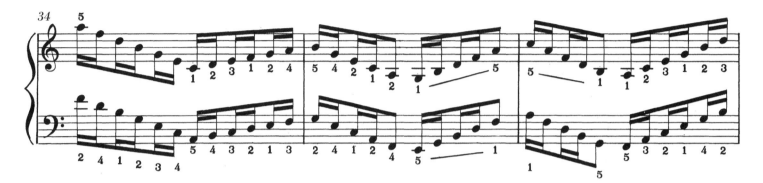

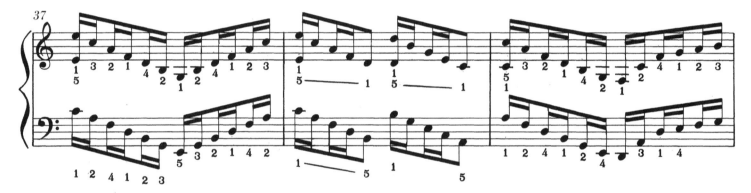

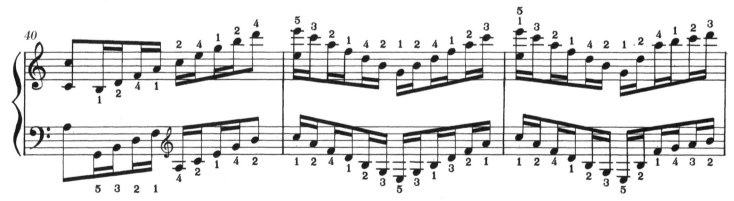

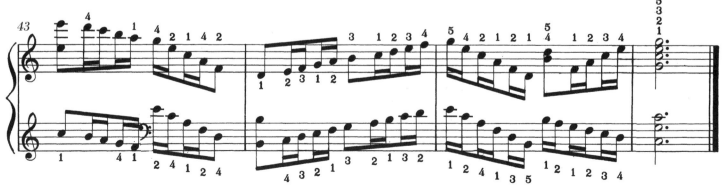

New York, 4 May 1984